AF207095

GENDER VIOLENCE

by Philip Wolny

BrightPoint Press

San Diego, CA

© 2025 BrightPoint Press
an imprint of ReferencePoint Press, Inc.
Printed in the United States

For more information, contact:
BrightPoint Press
PO Box 27779
San Diego, CA 92198
www.BrightPointPress.com

LIBRARY OF CONGRESS CATALOGING-IN-PUBLICATION DATA

Names: Wolny, Philip, author.
Title: Gender violence / by Philip Wolny.
Description: San Diego, CA: BrightPoint Press, [2025] | Series: Human rights at risk | Includes bibliographical references and index. | Audience: Grades 7-9
Identifiers: LCCN 2024004131 (print) | LCCN 2024004132 (eBook) | ISBN 9781678209261 (hardcover) | ISBN 9781678209278 (eBook)
Subjects: LCSH: Gender-based violence--Juvenile literature. | Gender-based violence--United States--Juvenile literature. | Women--Violence against--Juvenile literature. | Women--Violence against--United States--Juvenile literature.
Classification: LCC HV6250.4.W65 W6524 2025 (print) | LCC HV6250.4.W65 (eBook) | DDC 362.88082--dc23/eng/20240214
LC record available at https://lccn.loc.gov/2024004131
LC eBook record available at https://lccn.loc.gov/2024004132

CONTENTS

- Gender violence means harmful acts committed against a person or group because of their gender.

- Women and girls face gender violence everywhere in the world. As many as one in three are estimated to become victims in their lifetimes.

- Gender violence harms women and girls physically and mentally.

- According to the United Nations, about 81,000 women were intentionally killed worldwide in 2021.

- War, disease, and political problems usually increase the amount of gender violence any population of women experiences.

- As of September 2023, at least 162 nations had laws against domestic violence.

- Shelters are a big part of the fight against gender violence in the United States. They provide a safe bed to sleep in, therapy, legal and medical help, and opportunities to change the lives of abused women.

- Changing the attitudes of men, boys, and society through education is part of the ongoing fight to end gender violence everywhere.

GENDER VIOLENCE IN THE PUBLIC EYE

Rappers Megan Thee Stallion and Tory Lanez left a party in Los Angeles. It was July 12, 2020. They argued in the car. Finally, Megan left the car. Lanez fired a gun five times in her direction. One of the shots hit her foot.

Police arrived. They asked Megan about her injury. She told them she had stepped on broken glass. She did not report Lanez for shooting her. But he was arrested

When Megan Thee Stallion was a victim of gender violence in 2020, her case attracted a lot of media attention.

after police found the gun. Megan had to have surgery.

That August, Megan posted on Instagram Live. She admitted that Lanez had shot her. She said he and others had harassed her. Lanez and his team created fake email and social media accounts. They posed as Megan's record company to trick the media into believing Megan was lying. They created fake conversations between Lanez and Megan. On Lanez's next album, he accused her of lying.

In August 2023, Lanez was found guilty on three charges. One was assault with a firearm. Another was illegal possession of a firearm. The third charge was negligent discharge of a gun. He was sentenced to

One in three women have been affected by gender violence in their lifetimes.

10 years in prison. Megan Thee Stallion got justice. But many others do not.

WHAT IS GENDER VIOLENCE?

Megan and Lanez are famous rappers. That's why the shooting made the news. But violence against women and girls happens every day. It is known as gender violence or violence against women.

The European Commission sets human rights policies in Europe. It defines gender violence as "violence directed against a person because of that person's gender."[1] Women do commit violence against men. But most gender violence is committed by men and boys against women and girls.

Often stories of gender violence don't appear in the news. It happens on a lonely street or in the workplace. It can happen in people's homes. Gender violence kills about three women each day in the United States. But many people are working to end this human rights crisis.

Women walking home alone after dark may be targets for gender violence.

CHAPTER ONE

A WORLDWIDE ISSUE

Gender violence has a long history. It has been common in many cultures. Women traditionally had fewer rights than men. For a long time, men were usually not punished for harming women. Women were often afraid to report gender violence.

In modern times, many nations have passed laws to stop gender violence. Activists work to protect women and girls.

Educating young men about gender violence is one way to begin to change how women are treated in different cultures.

PROTECT YOUR DAUGHTER
EDUCATE YOUR SON
MOdest C
well Lit F
STILL N

But gender violence remains a serious human rights issue.

The World Health Organization (WHO) tracks violence against women. In 2021 it issued a report about the issue. It found that one in three women ages 15 to 49 had experienced violence.

TYPES OF GENDER VIOLENCE

Gender violence takes many forms. Domestic violence is the most common. This is violent behavior within the home. It usually involves the abuse of a partner. Abuse can be physical. It can also be psychological. This is when a person uses words or intimidation to harm a partner.

Femicide is the most serious form of gender violence. This is killing a woman

In cities around the world, people gather to protest violence against women.

just because of her gender. UN Women is part of the United Nations. A 2021 UN Women report found that 56 percent of murdered women were killed by a partner or family member.

Other forms of gender violence involve marriage. One example is forced marriage. Another is the marriage of children. Many countries now ban these things. But these marriages still happen around the world.

Child marriages are part of the culture in some countries. About 640 million of the women and girls alive in 2023 were married when they were younger than 18 years old.

In certain countries, particularly in Africa, groups also practice genital mutilation. This is the cutting or surgical removal of parts of girls' anatomy. As many as 200 million girls worldwide are victims of this practice.

WAR AND NATURAL DISASTERS

Gender violence increases during war and economic crisis. Women and children are affected by war in terrible ways. It breaks down the normal protections in a society. For example, police may not be around to stop crimes. This allows abusers to commit gender violence more easily.

Women in war-torn areas are at higher risk for gender violence.

Rape is one of the most common war crimes. Soldiers may even use it as a weapon of war. Refugees who escape war may still face gender violence. Refugee camps can be unsafe for women and girls. Gender violence is common in places that lack health care, housing, or security.

VIOLENCE IN EVERYDAY LIFE

Gender violence happens every day. Most often the person who assaults a woman is someone they know. It may be a partner, coworker, or friend.

Many women face harassment at work. Some careers are known for being male dominated. These fields include technology and banking. Such workplaces can be particularly hostile for women.

Women in other fields are at greater risk, too. These include construction, agriculture, and health care. Housekeepers and nannies are also vulnerable. These women often work alone. This increases the risk.

The threat of violence exists online, too. Women who speak out about social justice issues are often harassed. Journalists and video game streamers face threats, too. But harassment can happen to anyone. Sexist slurs and threats of violence and rape are common. Targeted women are

Staying Silent

Some workers in low-income jobs may not report gender violence. They worry that if they do, they might lose their jobs. Women with higher-paying jobs often do not report incidents at work, either. They worry that they will be punished or ignored.

sometimes **doxxed**. Victims may fear for their safety.

In 2017, Amnesty International noted this trend. "Online violence and abuse against women has become a far too common experience," the organization said. "More so, if you're a woman from a **minority** racial, ethnic, or religious background."[2]

THE MOST MARGINALIZED

All women experience gender violence. But women in **marginalized** groups are at greater risk. Poverty is one risk factor. Poor women often find it harder to escape abuse. Women may tolerate abuse to keep a job or place to live.

Women of specific ethnic or religious groups face higher risk, too. This is often

WHERE SEXUAL ASSAULT IS MOST LIKELY TO OCCUR

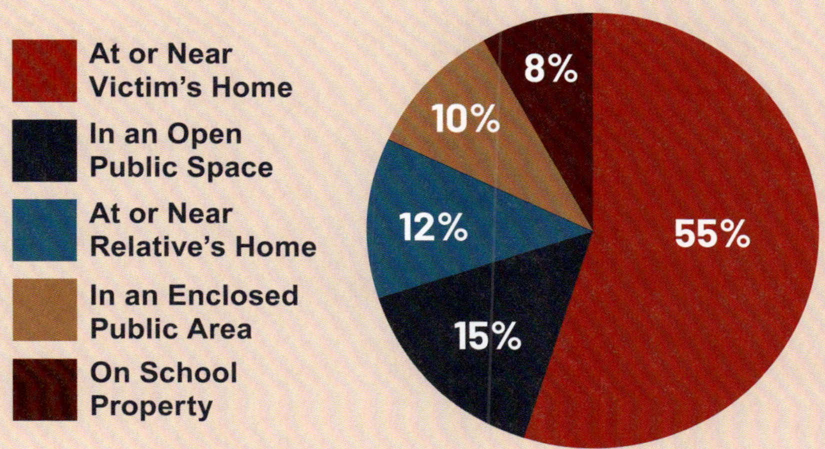

Source: Department of Justice, Office of Justice Programs, Bureau of Justice Statistics, "Female Victims of Sexual Violence, 1994–2010," 2013.

This pie chart shows where women are most likely to experience sexual assault.

due to **discrimination**. Women who identify as LGBTQ+ are at risk. Men sometimes target these women.

Women are the primary targets for gender violence. But they are not the cause of it. The people who do harm are responsible for this human rights crisis.

CHAPTER TWO

CAUSES AND EFFECTS OF GENDER VIOLENCE

The reasons for gender violence are often cultural. In many cultures, people believe men are better than women. Men learn that they should be aggressive. They may be taught that men should lead.

Boys may learn that men are always right. Many women also learn these attitudes. Such beliefs can make men think that hurting women is okay.

Those who support equal rights and safety for women are working to make their voices heard.

More cinnamon rolls
- Less gender roles.
SMASH THE
ATRIARCHY

PATRIARCHY

The idea that men are more important than women shapes a system called patriarchy. In this system, men control society. It is based on the belief that women are not smart enough to lead. In a patriarchy, people think women should do what men want. Often this means women can be only wives and mothers.

Elements of patriarchy exist in many cultures. The United States is not a patriarchy. But men tend to have more power in many areas of life. This can lead to a concept some people call *bro culture*. It is often tied to college **fraternities** and heavy drinking. Bro culture is sometimes linked to sexual assault and other kinds of gender violence.

Fritz Jolivain was in a fraternity at Boston University. He explained that bro culture isn't new. "I think the biggest pressure to be hyper masculine comes from societal **norms** that have been in place since ancient times," he said. "There has

Members of college fraternities may feel pressure from friends to treat women in ways they wouldn't if they were on their own.

always been this idea that men must act a certain way."[3]

In some traditional cultures, patriarchy is strong. These include tribes and religious

Women in demonstrations around the world are doing their part to raise awareness about femicide.

sects in parts of Africa, the Middle East, and Asia. These groups believe men have absolute power over women. Honor killings are still common. This is when families kill women who challenge men. Women may be killed for trying to work. They may be killed for shaming their family. The UN estimates that as many as 5,000 women are victims of honor killings each year.

THE EFFECTS OF GENDER VIOLENCE

Gender violence affects everyone in society. It hurts the women who are the victims of gender violence. They may suffer physically from abuse. Often they have emotional scars as well. Some women even die because of gender violence.

The UN estimates that around 81,000 women and girls were murdered in 2021. Many of these killings were believed to be gender motivated.

For those who survive, effects of gender violence can last a long time. Victims may experience depression or anxiety. Some may have thoughts of suicide. Many women have post-traumatic stress disorder (PTSD). This can cause headaches and tiredness. It can make sleep difficult. Stress from gender violence can also cause heart disease and diabetes.

The threat of gender violence even affects women who have not experienced it themselves. Many women worry about becoming victims. This threat affects choices they make every day. And if

The stress of being a victim of gender violence can cause mental and physical illnesses.

someone does harm them, they worry about being blamed.

Gender violence affects men and boys, too. UN Women reported on boys who saw

Young boys who grow up in a home with domestic violence suffer lasting effects.

their fathers hit their mothers. There were

lasting effects on these boys. They grew

up thinking partner violence was okay.

The cycle of violence may be passed from

fathers to sons.

Communities are affected by gender violence as well. Sexual violence can lead to unwanted pregnancies or sexually transmitted infections (STIs). And it can harm a woman's education and work life. Relationships can also be affected. These issues impact the health, economy, and well-being of a society.

Locked Down in Guatemala

During the COVID-19 pandemic, Guatemala experienced a rise in gender violence. Many women were stuck at home with their abusers. Silvia Trujillo reported in 2021, "We live here in a state that is incapable of protecting its women and where the political will to do so is lacking . . . violence against women is often not reported."

Source: Oliver Pieper, "In Guatemala, Women Fear for their Lives," DW.com, May 2, 2021. www.dw.com.

CHAPTER THREE

ENDING GENDER VIOLENCE INTERNATIONALLY

The Coalition to End Violence Against Women and Girls has called gender violence a global crisis. UN Women states that one in three women have been victims of violence. Activists are working with governments to change laws. As of September 2023, at least 162 nations had passed domestic violence laws. Also, 147 nations had passed laws against workplace sexual harassment.

Activists around the world take a stand against gender violence in the streets and in legislatures.

END
VIOLENCE
AGAINST
WOMEN
STOP
MALE
END

Activists have also worked with governments to help victims. One way is to provide services for women suffering from gender violence. This includes establishing health centers and shelters. These are safe spaces for women and children. They help people escape domestic violence.

WORKING TO END GENDER VIOLENCE

Equality Now (EN) works to prevent child marriages and **human trafficking**. It helps train police and government officials. They learn how to set up services to help women. EN also provides education. It hopes to change how men treat women. EN works with lawmakers. Since 1999, the group has worked in thirty-four nations.

It has helped change many laws that
discriminate against women.

In Uganda, UN Women works with
UGANET. This group works to secure
human rights for all. In 2020, it opened
a women's shelter in Kampala, Uganda.
Domestic violence had increased in

Shelters provide food, medical care, and a warm place to sleep for women who have survived gender violence.

Uganda during the COVID-19 pandemic. The shelter took in victims of violence and human trafficking. It provided women with a safe place to sleep. They also got medical and legal help.

A DANGEROUS PLACE FOR WOMEN

Afghanistan is one of the most dangerous countries in the world. It is especially unsafe for women. The country has experienced war and unrest for several decades. Since 2021, the Taliban has ruled Afghanistan. This is a religious **faction**. Its laws sharply restrict women's rights. The Taliban believes in a strict form of Islam. Its members punish anyone who violates the rules. One mother in Kabul, Afghanistan, talked to the

Women in Afghanistan follow rules set by the Taliban about what type of clothing they must wear.

United States Institute of Peace. She said the Taliban beat her fifth-grade daughter. They were punishing her for not covering her face.

In 1995, a group of activists formed the Afghan Women's Network (AWN). Mary Akrami founded the organization. Akrami opened one of the first women's shelters in Kabul. Akrami explained what it's like in her country. "Afghanistan is one of the hardest places for women to live," she said. "A large number of Afghan women experience violence. The women and men who raise their voices against these injustices and defend women's human rights risk their lives."[4]

In 2001, US troops and their allies invaded and removed the Taliban. In the

When the Taliban was not in power, girls in Afghanistan were allowed to go to school.

2000s and 2010s, women had more rights. Many girls started to go to school. Women were able to have jobs. But after US troops left the country in 2021, the Taliban regained power. They again limited women's rights. Akrami's group was forced to work in secret. It continues working to protect women.

Journalist Mahbouba Seraj is an AWN board member. She refused to leave Afghanistan when the Taliban took over.

She urged others everywhere to protect women's rights. She said, "What is happening to the women of Afghanistan can happen anywhere. . . . Women's rights being taken away from them is happening everywhere and if we are not careful, it will happen to all the women of the world."[5]

STANDING UP FOR GIRLS

In neighboring Pakistan, the Pakistani Taliban imposes strict rules on women and girls. Malala Yousafzai is a young activist. She was born in Mingora, Pakistan, in 1997. Her father was an education activist. He ran a school for girls in their village.

In 2008, the Taliban conquered the region where Yousafzai lived. The group banned music and television.

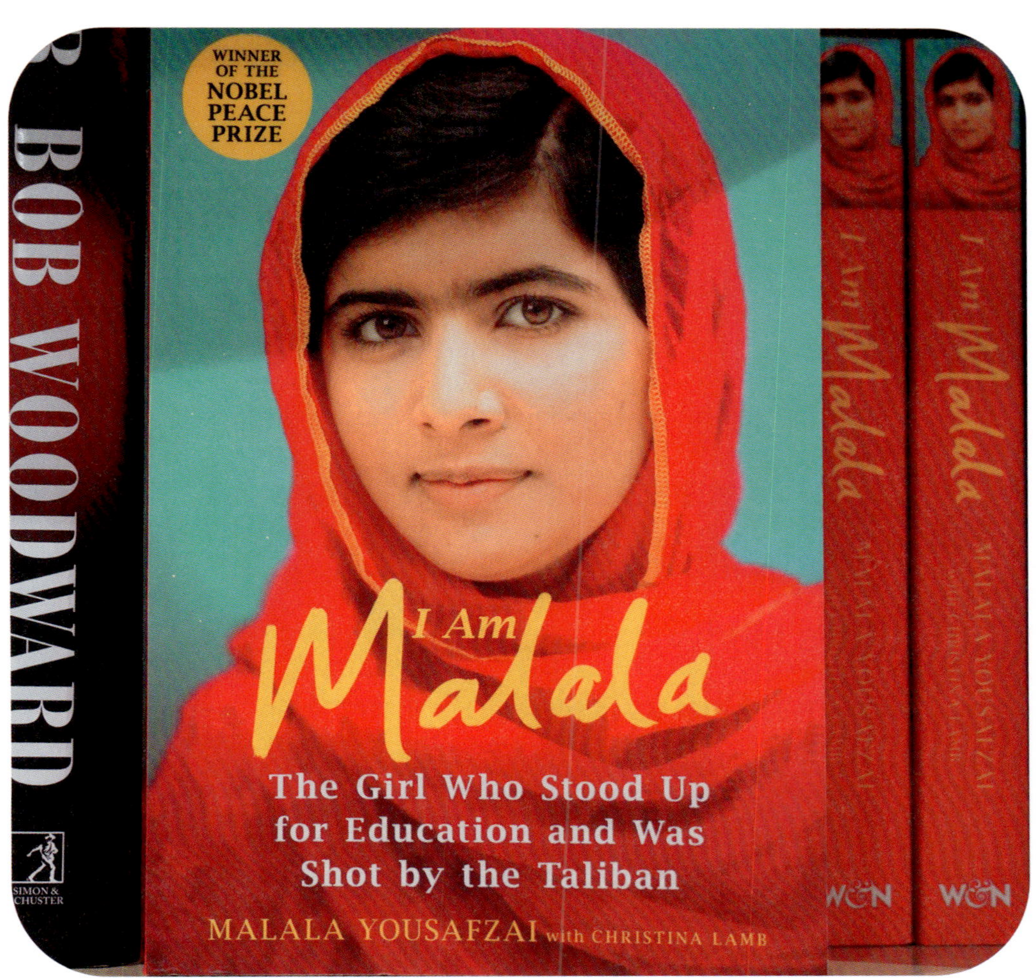

Malala Yousafzai published a book in 2013 about her attack, recovery, and fight for women's rights.

They also forced the girls' school to close. Malala believed these rules were unjust. She posted her thoughts on a blog run by the British Broadcasting Corporation. Her words later appeared in a documentary from the *New York Times*. This made Malala a target. She was on a bus in 2012 when a masked gunman boarded who shot her in the head. She survived and recovered. Her story was shared by media around the world.

This terrifying experience made her stronger. She wrote a biography. She also appeared in a movie about her story. Malala won the Nobel Peace Prize in 2014.

Malala Yousafzai continues to fight for women and girls to have the right to an education. In 2023, Yousafzai attended the Independent Spirit Awards.

She continues to speak out. Her father helped her set up the Malala Fund. This charity helps promote girls' education in many parts of the world.

ENDING GENDER VIOLENCE IN THE UNITED STATES

The Violence Against Women Act (VAWA) was passed in 1994. President Bill Clinton signed it into law. It established the federal Office on Violence Against Women (OVW). The OVW provides money to states to take action against sexual assault and stalking. Nonprofit organizations can also apply for OVW money. These resources support women's shelters

Joe Biden was a senator in 1994 when the VAWA was first signed into law. He worked to strengthen the law in the years that followed, including after becoming president in 2021.

VICE PRESIDENT OF THE UNITED STATES
E PLURIBUS UNUM

and rape crisis centers. The money also provides education on gender violence.

There is evidence that the VAWA is working. The US Department of Justice says that domestic violence fell by 64 percent between 1994 and 2010. In March 2022, President Joe Biden signed the VAWA Reauthorization Act. This revised law funds housing, prevention programs, and legal assistance for survivors. It also includes protections for LGBTQ+ and Native people. As a result of this law, gender violence incidents are treated as serious crimes.

SHELTERS

Shelters help women escape partner violence. Many victims are stuck in abusive homes. They cannot afford a hotel. Emergency shelters can help. For many, shelters are the first step in escaping abuse. Some shelters are run by nonprofits. Others are run by the government.

Women who flee domestic abuse often rely on shelters to help them begin a new life.

Therapists help victims of gender violence cope with the effects of their abuse.

In 1976, Barbara Moore started taking domestic violence victims into her home. This was rare at the time. Moore made it more acceptable to talk about gender violence. Her shelter later became Harbor House of Central Florida. Over the years, it grew into one of Florida's largest women's shelters.

Harbor House has an emergency shelter with 110 beds. It is open 24 hours a day. Counselors work with victims. They help them find new homes and jobs. Women receive trauma therapy and medical care. Harbor House trains first responders as well. Emergency staff and government officials learn how to recognize abuse. They are taught how to best help victims.

PREVENTION AND RESOURCES

Many other organizations work to end gender violence. The National Resource Center on Domestic Violence (NRCDV) is one of the largest. The NRCDV performs research and trains professionals who help victims. It collects statistics and uses this information to influence lawmakers.

Hotlines provide a safe number for women to call to report abuse and learn about resources.

The data is also used to educate students, teachers, and the greater community.

Other groups help specific communities. For example, the National Indigenous

Women's Resource Center helps Native communities. Esperanza United works to end gender violence in the Latino community. The Rape, Abuse & Incest National Network (RAINN) helps sexual assault victims. RAINN runs the National Sexual Assault Hotline. This is a phone number that victims of sexual assault can call for support 24 hours a day.

Another emergency resource is the National Domestic Violence Hotline. This hotline took its first call in 1996. In 2007, it launched Love Is Respect. This organization provides support through a website and hotline to young adults ages 13 through 26 in all fifty states. It helps teens who experience dating abuse.

CHANGING HEARTS AND MINDS

Education is a key tool for ending gender violence. Educational programs teach young people how to recognize it. Students learn how words and attitudes can be harmful. These programs also provide examples of healthy relationships.

There are programs for students of all ages, from elementary school through college. For example, Johns Hopkins University offers Bystander Intervention Training (BIT). Students learn how to tell if a fellow student is in danger. They also learn how they can help stop an incident.

Education and awareness is a big part of prevention. Michael Flood researches gender and interpersonal violence. He notes that most men and boys do not commit

Education about how to prevent gender violence can help break the cycle of abuse.

violence against women. But he points out that men play a big role in ending gender violence. Flood says, "We must examine our own behavior and ensure that we treat the women and girls in our lives with nonviolence, respect, and care. . . . When a male friend makes derogatory comments, such as claiming that some women ask to be raped or that some women bring violence upon themselves, we should speak up. Similarly, if we witness men around us treating women disrespectfully, with sexism or hostility, we must address it."[6] Talking openly about gender violence can bring about change.

THE ME TOO MOVEMENT

Activist Tarana Burke first used the phrase "Me Too" in 2006. Burke was a survivor of sexual violence. She used Me Too to connect with young girls who had similar experiences.

On October 15, 2017, actress Alyssa Milano posted on the social media site Twitter, now X. Her post read, "If you've

Tarana Burke has been an activist since her teens. She works to help young Black girls who have experienced gender violence.

been sexually harassed or assaulted write 'me too' as a reply to this tweet."[7] Over the next 24 hours, thousands of people shared the post. It inspired a hashtag, #MeToo. This hashtag was used more than 19 million times in the following year. Women shared experiences with gender violence. They talked about harassment at work and sexual assault. For many, it was the first time they had talked about these events.

During this movement, many women accused powerful men of sexual misconduct. Some of these men lost their jobs. Their reputations suffered. The movement inspired women to name their attackers and harassers. It helped women

Getting Justice

In October 2017, news reports came out about Hollywood producer Harvey Weinstein. Weinstein was accused of sexually assaulting several women. The crimes happened over many years. The Me Too Movement inspired Weinstein's victims to come forward. By 2023, Weinstein was convicted of three different sexual crimes. His longest prison sentence was 23 years.

support each other. Many realized they weren't alone.

A LONG JOURNEY AHEAD

Public awareness is only part of the struggle against gender violence. Education is another important piece of this fight. A new generation has the chance to change harmful attitudes toward women.

Activists and lawmakers continue to push for change. They are addressing sexist laws and systems worldwide. The fight against gender violence continues.

GLOSSARY

discrimination

the act of treating people differently because of their race, gender, ethnicity, or religion

doxxed

posting private information about a person on social media or in other public forums

faction

a party or group that disagrees with and breaks away from a larger group

fraternities

mens' organizations most often associated with colleges that are formed for social purposes

human trafficking

forcing or tricking someone to work for free or perform a sex act

marginalized

discriminated against in some way

minority

a part of the population that is treated differently than the rest

norms

rules for acceptable behavior

SOURCE NOTES

INTRODUCTION: GENDER VIOLENCE IN THE PUBLIC EYE

1. Quoted in "What Is Gender-Based Violence?," *European Commission*, n.d. www. commission.europa.eu.

CHAPTER ONE: A WORLDWIDE ISSUE

2. Quoted in "What Is Online Violence and Abuse Against Women," *Amnesty International*, November 20, 2017. www.amnesty.org.

CHAPTER TWO: CAUSES AND EFFECTS OF GENDER VIOLENCE

3. Quoted in Kyler Sumter, "What We Mean When We Say 'Bro Culture,'" *USA Today*, June 7, 2017. www.usatoday.com.

CHAPTER THREE: ENDING GENDER VIOLENCE INTERNATIONALLY

4. Quoted in "In Her Own Words: Mary Akrami," *Women's Peace & Humanitarian Fund*, n.d. www.wphfund.org.

5. Quoted in "In the Words of Mahbouba Seraj: 'We Are the Hope, We are the Power Keeping Afghanistan Together," *UN Women*, August 12, 2022. www.unwomen.org.

CHAPTER FOUR: ENDING GENDER VIOLENCE IN THE UNITED STATES

6. Quoted in "Interview with Professor Michael Flood: How Men Can Take Action Against Violence Against Women in Their Daily Lives," *RAJA-Danièle Marcovici Foundation*, July 7, 2023. www.fondation-raja-marcovici.com.

7. Quoted in Mary Pflum, "A Year Ago, Alyssa Milano Started a Conversation About #MeToo. These Women Replied," *NBC News*, October 15, 2018. www.nbcnews.com.

FOR FURTHER RESEARCH

BOOKS

Winifred Conkling, *Votes for Women!: American Suffragists and the Battle for the Ballot*. New York: Algonquin Young Readers, 2020.

Barbara Krasner (ed.), *Toxic Masculinity*. New York: Greenhaven Publishing, 2020.

Gail Radley, *Modern Slavery and Human Trafficking*. San Diego, CA: BrightPoint Press, 2025.

INTERNET SOURCES

Oliver Pieper, "In Guatemala, Women Fear for Their Lives," *DW.com*, May 2, 2021. www.dw.com.

"What Is Gender-Based Violence—And How Do We Prevent It?" *Rescue.org*, August 22, 2023. www.rescue.org.

"What Is Online Violence and Abuse Against Women?" *Amnesty International*, November 20, 2017. www.amnesty.org.

WEBSITES

National Coalition Against Domestic Violence (NCADV)
www.ncadv.org

The National Coalition Against Domestic Violence works to help victims and survivors of domestic violence. It amplifies their voices to press for a change in culture to prevent gender violence.

Rape, Abuse & Incest National Network (RAINN)
www.rainn.org

RAINN is an American nonprofit organization that works to prevent sexual assault, assist survivors, and seek justice for victims. It runs the National Sexual Assault Hotline and the Department of Defense Safe Helpline, which assists military victims of abuse.

UN Women
www.unwomen.org

UN Women is an organization that is part of the United Nations (UN). It is the main UN entity that focuses on fighting for gender equality and the rights of women and girls. It also fights against gender violence around the world.

INDEX

IMAGE CREDITS

Cover: © Imageplotter/Alamy Live News/Alamy

5: © Vincenzo Lullo/Shutterstock Images

7: © Featureflash Photo Agency/Shutterstock Images

9: © STEKLO/Shutterstock Images

11: © Viacheslav Rubel/Shutterstock Images

13: © Vincenzo Lullo/Shutterstock Images

15: © Bohemian Photography/Shutterstock Images

16: © Riccardo Mayer/Shutterstock Images

17: © quetions123/Shutterstock Images

21: © Red Line Editorial

23: © D. Busquets/Shutterstock Images

25: © Jeremy Liebman/Shutterstock Images

26: © Dutchmen Photography/Shutterstock Images

29: © fizkes/Shutterstock Images

30: © DimaBerlin/Shutterstock Images

33: © JessicaGirvan/Shutterstock Images

35: © addkm/Shutterstock Images

37: © timsimages.uk/Shutterstock Images

39: © Solmaz Daryani/Shutterstock Images

41: © Dfree/Shutterstock Images

43: © SN040288/Shutterstock Images

45: © Lev Radin/Shutterstock Images

47: © Monkey Business Images/Shutterstock Images

48: © Prostock-Studio/Shutterstock Images

50: © F01 PHOTO/Shutterstock Images

53: © Studio Romantic/Shutterstock Images

55: © Lev Radin/Shutterstock Images

ABOUT THE AUTHOR

Philip Wolny is a writer, editor, father, and native New Yorker now living in Central Florida with his wife and daughter. As a father and husband, he remains hopeful for a world where gender equality is a reality and gender violence is largely a thing of the past.